URSA

SPACE REVEALED

EARTH & THE MOON

by
Claudia Martin

Minneapolis, Minnesota

Credits

Cover and title page, © mozZz/Adobe Stock and © NASA Goddard/NASA; 5-Apr, © MelvinL/Adobe Stock; 6MR, © designua/Adobe Stock; 6BR, © Vadim Sadovski/NASA/Shutterstock; 7, © Goddard Space Flight Center/Arizona State University/NASA; 8, © Mikkel Juul Jensen/Science Photo Library; 9, © Science Photo Library/Alamy; 10, © Destina/Adobe Stock; 11, © Hellen888/Shutterstock; 12, © Yarr65/Adobe Stock; 13M, © GraphicsRF/Adobe Stock; 13BR, © Maygutyak/Adobe Stock; 14, © Manuel Mata/Adobe Stock; 15, © VectorMine/Adobe Stock; 16, © VectorMine/Adobe Stock; 17, © VectorMine/Adobe Stock; 17BR, © Simon's passion 4 Travel/Adobe Stock; 18, © Anastasiia Malinich/Adobe Stock; 19, © Macrovector/Adobe Stock and © Peter Hermes Furian/Adobe Stock; 20MR, © Lukasz Janyst/Adobe Stock; 20BR, © blueringmedia/Adobe Stock; 21, © Katrina Brown/Shutterstock; 22, © Designua/Shutterstock; 22BR, © Near D Krasaesom/NASA/Shutterstock 23M, © Aldona Griskeviciene/Shutterstock; 23BR, © Mikkel Juul Jensen/Science Photo Library; 24, © rktz/Shutterstock; 25, © Susan Natoli/Shutterstock; 26, © Nazarii/Adobe Stock; 27, © PRILL/Shutterstock; 28MR, © Matis75/Shutterstock and © Siberian Art/Shutterstock; 28BR, © GSFC/Arizona State University/NASA; 29, © NASA images/Shutterstock; 30, © Mikkel Juul Jensen/Science Photo Library; 31M, © Primož Cigler/Shutterstock 31B, © Vadim Petrakov/Shutterstock 32, © 315202645/Adobe Stock; 33, © Mark Garlick/Science Photo Library/Alamy; 34, © NASA; 35, © Ames/NASA; 36, © blueringmedia/Adobe Stock; 37, © Siberian Art/Adobe Stock; 38, © NASA; 39, © NASA; 40, © Apollo 14 Crew/NASA; 41, © NASA; 42-43, © NASA; 44, © Destina/Adobe Stock; 45TR, © Primož Cigler/Shutterstock; 45BR, © Lukasz Janyst/Adobe Stock; 47, © Mikkel Juul Jensen/Science Photo Library

Bearport Publishing Company Product Development Team
President: Jen Jenson; Director of Product Development: Spencer Brinker; Managing Editor: Allison Juda; Associate Editor: Naomi Reich; Associate Editor: Tiana Tran; Art Director: Colin O'Dea; Designer: Kim Jones; Designer: Kayla Eggert; Product Development Assistant: Owen Hamlin

Statement on Usage of Generative Artificial Intelligence
Bearport Publishing remains committed to publishing high-quality nonfiction books. Therefore, we restrict the use of generative AI to ensure accuracy of all text and visual components pertaining to a book's subject. See BearportPublishing.com for details.

Library of Congress Cataloging-in-Publication Data is available at www.loc.gov or upon request from the publisher.

ISBN: 979-8-89232-078-8 (hardcover)
ISBN: 979-8-89232-610-0 (paperback)
ISBN: 979-8-89232-211-9 (ebook)

© 2025 Arcturus Holdings Limited
This edition is published by arrangement with Arcturus Publishing Limited.

North American adaptations © 2025 Bearport Publishing Company. All rights reserved. No part of this publication may be reproduced in whole or in part, stored in any retrieval system, or transmitted in any form or by any means, electronic, mechanical, photocopying, recording, or otherwise, without written permission from the publisher. Bearport Publishing is a division of Chrysalis Education Group.

For more information, write to Bearport Publishing, 5357 Penn Avenue South, Minneapolis, MN 55419.

CONTENTS

Our Home 4
Earth Basics 6
How Earth and the Moon Were Born 8
Earth's Structure 10
The Moving Mantle 12
Pangea 14
Earth's Magnetic Field 16
Earth's Orbit and Seasons 18
An Earth Day 20
Earth's Atmosphere 22
Water on Earth 24
Life on Earth 26
Moon Basics 28
Phases of the Moon 30
The Lunar Surface 32
The Moon's Atmosphere 34
The Moon and Earth's Tides 36
Landing on the Moon 38
Walking on the Moon 40
Side by Side 42

Review and Reflect 44
Glossary 46
Read More 47
Learn More Online 47
Index 48

OUR HOME

Our planet and its moon have a special relationship. They began forming just a few million years apart, during the turbulent beginnings of our solar system. They evolved together for billions of years, culminating in the moon affecting life on Earth and providing a stepping stone for space exploration.

Earth and the moon share many of the same traits and composition. They are also, however, very different. Where Earth is colorful and full of life, the pale moon is dull and quiet. The moon constantly orbits Earth, traveling with the planet on its own course around the sun.

Earth and the moon have been together for about 4.5 billion years. They are expected to remain together for about another 10 billion years—for as long as the sun continues to exist and provide warmth and light. Over time, they may both slow down a bit. Earth will rotate less rapidly and the moon will circle Earth more slowly. Someday in the distant future, the moon may even match its orbit's pace to Earth's rotation. Then, it would shine over the same spot on Earth for the remainder of their days.

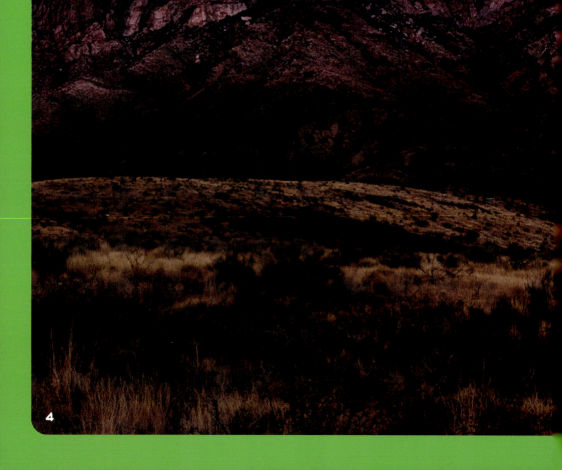

A super moon rises over towering mountains in New Mexico.

EARTH BASICS

Earth is the largest of the inner planets. The third planet from our sun, it receives enough warmth from the star for water to flow on its surface. If Earth were hotter, water would boil. If it were colder, the planet's water would freeze. Without water, there would be no life. As far as we currently know, Earth is the only planet in the universe that is home to life.

As Earth orbits the sun, it also rotates on its own axis, an imaginary line that runs through the planet's core from its north pole to its south pole. Earth rotates eastward, with each rotation taking 24 hours. The side of Earth that is facing the sun experiences day, while the other experiences night. Earth's axis is tilted slightly in relation to its orbit around the sun. This means that apart from at the equator, no place experiences an even split of day and night all the time.

It takes 365.25 days for Earth to orbit the sun. Since this is longer than the 365-day year we use in our calendars, every four years we have a leap year with 366 days to keep pace. The tilt of Earth's axis creates seasons. When the north pole is tilted toward the sun, the planet's northern hemisphere experiences summer while the southern hemisphere has winter.

Earth's rocky crust is broken into several large pieces, called tectonic plates. They are always moving very slowly on the partly melted rock below. This movement can make mountains and valleys. It can send the melted rock up to the surface through volcanoes.

Earth's major tectonic plates

Earth

Type: Terrestrial planet
Size: 7,918 miles (12,742 km) across
Mass: The same as 0.000003 suns
Moons: 1
Year: 365.25 days
Day: 24 hours
Surface temperature: -129 to 134 degrees Fahrenheit (-89 to 57 degrees Celsius)
Average distance from the sun: 93 million miles (150 million km)

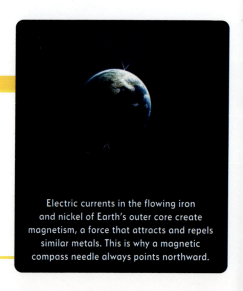

Electric currents in the flowing iron and nickel of Earth's outer core create magnetism, a force that attracts and repels similar metals. This is why a magnetic compass needle always points northward.

This photograph of Earth was taken by the *Lunar Reconnaissance Orbiter* robotic spacecraft from just above the moon.

HOW EARTH AND THE MOON WERE BORN

Earth is about 4.5 billion years old. The planet began to form soon after the sun first blazed to life. The sun's birth was the result of the explosion of a distant star. That star's violent death disturbed a thick cloud of gas and dust floating in space and caused it to start pulling together into a clump.

The clump that would become the sun began to grow within the cloud of gas. As it grew, its gravitational pull increased and it began to attract more matter, forming into a spinning sphere. The pressure within the core of the sphere became so intense that the atoms of gas collided with one another and began to fuse, releasing energy in the form of light and heat. The star known as our sun was born.

Dust continued to swirl around the new star, and eventually this matter also began to form into clumps of rock and metal. As the clumps grew, their increasing gravity set them spinning and shaped them into spheres. These became our solar system's planets and moons.

Earth was a spinning ball so hot that at first it was almost completely molten magma. As the planet cooled, it began to form layers. Surrounding the core of molten metal were solid and molten rocks. This was all covered by a rocky crust.

A few million years after it formed, Earth was struck by a Mars-sized object. The debris created by this collision was shaped into a ball by gravity and began to orbit our planet. This was the first appearance of the moon in our night sky. Because it was formed by debris from Earth, the moon shares many of the same elements, minerals, and metals found on our planet.

Earth and the Moon

Earth's age: 4.54 billion years
Planetary type: Terrestrial
Earth's size: 7,918 miles (12,742 km) across
Earth's average distance from the sun:
93 million miles (150 million km)
Moon's age: 4.51 billion years
Moon's size: 2,160 miles (3,476 km) across
Moon's average distance from Earth:
238,856 miles (384,402 km)

The moon probably formed when a planet that astronomers call Theia, crashed into Earth.

This illustration shows the stages in the formation of Earth and the moon. Around 3.8 billion years ago, liquid water condensed on the surface of Earth, and its atmosphere formed. Stable continents formed about 2.5 billion years ago.

EARTH'S STRUCTURE

Earth was made of rocks and metal so superheated that they were melted. While the planet's surface gradually cooled to form a rocky crust, much of its core still remains molten. In fact, Earth's inner core is nearly as hot as the surface of the sun.

As Earth cooled, its dense metals, such as nickel and iron, melted and sank to the center of the planet. Some of the metals became squeezed so tightly that they formed into the planet's solid inner core. This part of the planet is surrounded by the outer core, a layer of still-molten metal. Wrapped around both parts of the core is a very thick layer of heated rock known as the mantle. Some of this rock remains solid, but some of it is hot enough to melt into flowing magma.

The outside of the planet is covered by a thin and cool surface layer of solid rock called the crust. There are two kinds of crust: continental and oceanic.

Continental crust is what forms Earth's continents and most of its islands. It is the ground beneath our feet, supporting our homes, skyscrapers, and roads. The continental crust is about 20 to 45 miles (32 to 72 km) thick. The oceanic crust extends beneath the seafloor about 3 to 6 miles (5 to 10 km). While oceanic crust is much thinner than continental crust, it is also more densely packed.

Much of Earth's crust is covered by plants, landforms, and human construction. But whenever you stand on the sand of a desert or hike on a rocky mountain, you are in direct contact with our planet's crust.

Earth's Layers

Depth of inner core: 3,200 to 3,963 miles (5,150 to 6,378 km)
Temperature of inner core: 9,700°F (5,400°C)
Depth of outer core: 1,795 to 3,200 miles (2,890 to 5,150 km)
Temperature of outer core: 9,932°F (5,500°C)
Depth of mantle: 45 to 1,795 miles (70 to 2,890 km)
Temperature of mantle: 6,690°F (3,700°C)
Depth of crust: 0 to 45 miles (0 to 70 km)
Average temperature of crust: 57°F (14°C)

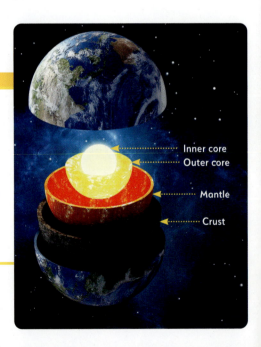

10

Between 30 and 70 million years ago, the plates in Earth's crust began pushing upward, forming the Colorado Plateau. Then about 5 million years ago, the Colorado River began wearing away the rock, carving out the Grand Canyon.

THE MOVING MANTLE

More than 500 million years after Earth first formed out of spinning, superheated gas and metal, the planet was still cooling down. As it cooled, the upper mantle and crust were broken up into tectonic plates.

Earth's huge tectonic plates float very slowly upon the molten parts of the mantle at a rate of about 1 to 6 inches (2 to 15 cm) a year. There are places all over the world where two plates meet each other. Depending on their movement, this meeting can dramatically change the landscape, creating mountains, valleys, or ocean ridges and trenches.

Volcanoes on land can form when a thin but heavy oceanic plate slides beneath a thicker continental plate. The oceanic plate moves into Earth's mantle, and some of its rock melts into magma. This extremely hot liquid rock then forces its way to the surface. Once it bursts through openings in Earth's crust, it is known as lava. Underwater volcanoes can form when two oceanic plates spread apart, creating cracks on the seafloor. Magma from Earth's mantle rises up to fill these cracks.

Whenever tectonic plates make contact with one another, the collision can result in an earthquake. As the plates grind together and get stuck, pressure builds. This pressure is released when the plates become unstuck, causing sudden and sometimes extremely violent shaking.

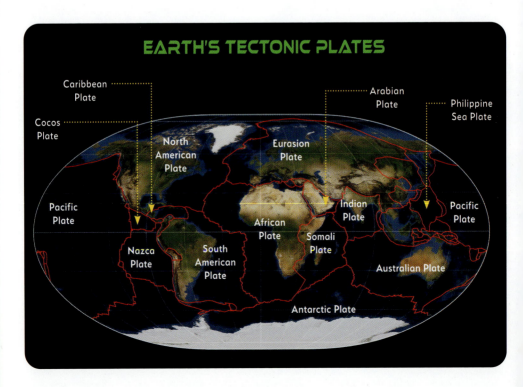

TYPES OF PLATE BOUNDARIES

Convergent Boundary
When two plates come together, it is known as a convergent boundary. This impact can cause one or both plates to buckle up into a mountain range. One of the plates may bend downward. A chain of volcanoes often forms at these boundaries, and earthquakes are common.

Divergent Boundary
A divergent boundary occurs when two tectonic plates move away from each other. Here, earthquakes are common, and magma rises to form new crust. Most divergent boundaries are located underwater, but they can occur on land, too.

Transform Boundary
When two plates slide past one another, it is known as a transform plate boundary. Rocks at the fault line, or where plates meet, are crushed and cracked. Earthquakes are common along these faults.

Earth's Highs and Lows

Subduction is when tectonic plates slide above and below each other. This process has created both Earth's highest place and its lowest point. Mount Everest is 29,000 feet (8,800 m) tall and continues to grow as the Indo-Australian plate slides below and pushes up on the Eurasian plate. The Mariana Trench lies almost 7 miles (11 km) beneath the Pacific Ocean and was formed by the Mariana plate pushing down on the Pacific Plate.

Mount Everest is Earth's tallest mountain above sea level. Each year, hundreds of climbers attempt the dangerous and difficult journey to the mountain's summit.

PANGEA

The movement of Earth's tectonic plates is a powerful force. It reshapes the landscape with every bump, slide, and collision. Over time, shifting plates and the rifts they cause can even move entire landmasses around the globe.

About 300 million years ago, North America, South America, Europe, Africa, Asia, Oceania, and Antarctica were all connected. Scientists have named this massive supercontinent Pangea, meaning all, entire, or whole. Over hundreds of millions of years, tectonic plate movement had slowly merged previous landmasses together. First, the continents of Laurentia (a portion of modern-day North America) and Baltic (Eastern Europe) merged along with several smaller landmasses to form Euramerica. Eventually, this continent collided with another that included present-day Africa, Antarctica, Australia, India, and South America. Finally, with the additional merging of Siberia into the growing supercontinent, Pangea was complete.

Yet what plate tectonics can join together, they can also pull apart. Pangea lasted for about 120 million years. Then, where plates met and made contact with one another, fissures began to appear. These cracks began to separate the landmass into northwestern Africa, North America, and South America. Magma from Earth's mantle began bubbling up through the fissures, and a volcanic rift zone developed. Amid volcanic eruptions, the formerly connected continents were pushed apart. Next, Africa, Antarctica, and South America pulled away from one another. The Indian subcontinent then separated from Antarctica and Australia. In the final stage of Pangea's breakup, North America separated from Europe, while Australia split off from Antarctica. India drifted away from Madagascar before joining with Eurasia, a violent collision that gave rise to the Himalayas and the highest mountain peaks in the world.

The Supercontinent Cycle

Pangea was only the most recent supercontinent in Earth's history. The continents we know today have come together and split apart at least three times and are still moving due to plate tectonics. Africa is slowly colliding with southern Europe, while Australia is moving toward southeast Asia. In the next 250 million years, North and South America, Africa, and Eurasia are expected to fuse together again, creating a whole new supercontinent.

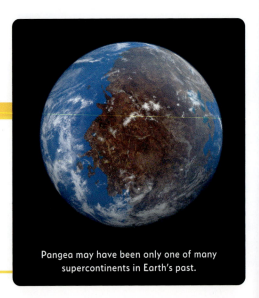

Pangea may have been only one of many supercontinents in Earth's past.

14

CONTINENTAL DRIFT

Continental drift was the theory that Earth's land began as the supercontinent Pangea, which broke into smaller continents that drifted into their modern places. Today, the concept of drifting has been replaced with plate tectonics to fully explain the movements. We also now know that many other landmass formations came before Pangea.

Pangea
(About 300 million years ago)

Laurasia and Gondwana
(About 200 million years ago)

Today

15

EARTH'S MAGNETIC FIELD

Earth is the only planet in our solar system that can sustain life. One of the things that makes life on our planet possible is the fact that Earth generates an electromagnetic field around itself. This energy shields the planet from dangerous particles flying through space.

The extreme heat of Earth's inner core keeps the liquid iron and nickel of the outer core in constant motion, while the planet's rotation creates a whirlpool-like flow. This flowing metal generates an electrical current that is hundreds of miles wide and moving at thousands of miles an hour. This massive electrical current generates a protective magnetic field that extends outward into space around Earth.

The sun continuously emits a stream of charged particles from its outer atmosphere. This is known as the solar wind. Earth's magnetic field shields us from these charged protons and electrons. It forces the radiation to flow around Earth, bouncing it out beyond our atmosphere, where it is trapped in donut-shaped belts of the magnetic field that surround Earth. These belts can also absorb the solar flares and storms that could cause radio, electronic, and power blackouts.

If the magnetic field were not around Earth to repel the solar wind, the charged particles would hurt the atmosphere, removing the oxygen we need in order to breathe and have water on the planet. This is what happened to Mars, which lost its magnetic field about 4 billion years ago. Solar winds stripped away most of the planet's atmosphere, similar to the way wind blows sand away. The atmosphere on Mars is now 100 times thinner than the one around Earth. This means that there is very little oxygen, and any water that may exist on its surface cannot last long, making it a very dry, barren planet.

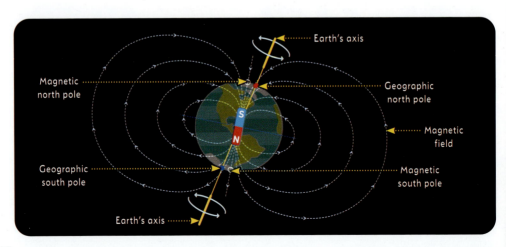

16

AURORA FORMATION

Auroras form when charged particles from solar flares or ejected gas are carried to Earth's atmosphere by the solar wind. When these particles interact with our planet's magnetic field, they slam into oxygen and nitrogen in the thin, upper atmosphere. This creates brilliant ribbons of color.

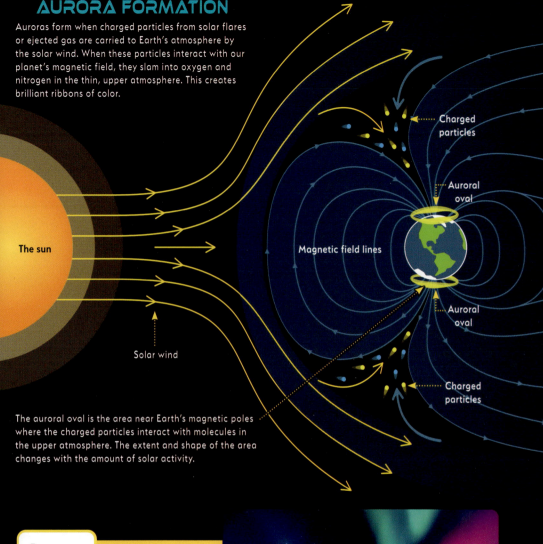

The auroral oval is the area near Earth's magnetic poles where the charged particles interact with molecules in the upper atmosphere. The extent and shape of the area changes with the amount of solar activity.

Auroras

Solar winds and Earth's magnetic field work together to create one of nature's most awe-inspiring spectacles—auroras. When solar winds strike the magnetic field, some of the charged particles become trapped in our atmosphere, where they interact with different types of gas molecules. When the particles interact with oxygen, they give off green or red light. When they mix with nitrogen, they create a blue or reddish-purple color.

Aurora borealis, also known as the northern lights, are seen close to the pole in the northern hemisphere. The similar display seen in the southern hemisphere is called the aurora australis.

EARTH'S ORBIT AND SEASONS

Ever since Earth was just a swirling disk of gas and dust, it has orbited the sun. Moving at more than 66,000 miles per hour (106,000 kph), Earth takes a little more than 365 days to complete its oval-shaped path around the sun. This amount of time is what we call a year.

Earth does not spin straight up and down relative to its orbit. Instead, it is tilted on an axis. This means that certain parts of Earth are pointed to the sun at different times of the year. During a portion of Earth's orbit, the northern hemisphere is tilted toward the sun, giving it more daylight hours and warmer temperatures. The summer solstice for this hemisphere is the moment when the north pole reaches its greatest tilt toward the sun and marks the beginning of summer. At this same time, the south pole is tilted farthest away from the sun, and the southern hemisphere experiences less daylight and the cooler temperatures of winter. The spring and fall equinoxes are the two points in the year when the sun shines directly on Earth's equator, giving both the northern and southern hemispheres the same amount of daylight, about 12 hours in each.

Summer

Winter

JUNE 20 OR 21 SOLSTICE

The Earth Year

Speed of Earth's orbit: 66,620 mph (107,200 kph)
Time to complete one orbit: 365.25 days
Solstices:
   June 20 or 21: (northern hemisphere's summer and southern hemisphere's winter)
   December 21 or 22: (northern hemisphere's winter and southern hemisphere's summer)
Equinoxes:
   About March 21: (northern hemisphere's spring and southern hemisphere's fall
   About September 23: (northern hemisphere's fall and southern hemisphere's spring)

CHANGING SEASONS ON EARTH

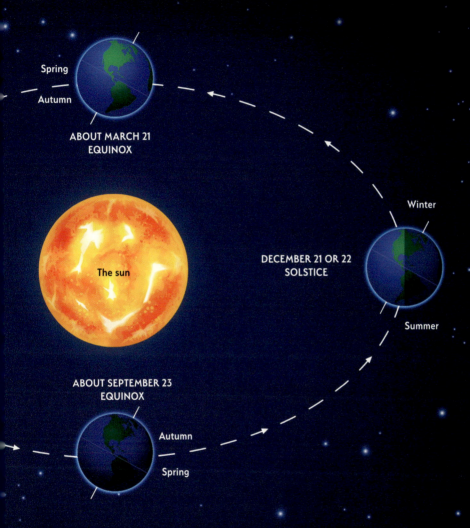

Because each orbit is one-quarter of a day longer than a 365-day year, every four years we have to add a full day—February 29—to our calendar. This is known as a leap year, with the 29th known as leap day. If we didn't add this day every four years, our calendars would fall out of sync with Earth's orbit. Over time, our seasons would no longer fall within their usual months.

AN EARTH DAY

Speeding through space and circling the sun in a year is not the only rapid-motion journey Earth takes. Our planet also rotates on its axis. This single rotation takes 24 hours to complete, making a full day on Earth.

Earth spins on its axis at about 1,000 mph (1,600 kph). As it makes its way around, almost every part of its surface faces the sun at some point. When a portion of Earth's surface spins toward the sun, the area experiences daylight. As it turns away from the sun, it enters darkness. If Earth did not rotate in this way, half of the planet would always be facing the sun and be unbearably hot and bright. The other half would forever be in deeply frozen darkness.

For much of human history, people believed that the sun and stars visible in the night sky rotated around Earth, which remained fixed in the center of the universe. Because the sun appeared to rise in the east and set in the west, people assumed the sun was moving, not Earth. It was not until Nicolaus Copernicus more accurately described a sun-centered solar system in 1543 that people began to understand and accept that Earth orbited the sun. Copernicus showed that the revolution and Earth's rotation on its axis made the year and its seasons. People realized the sun did not move around Earth as it rose and set. Instead, Earth spun to face the sun and turn away again within a 24-hour period.

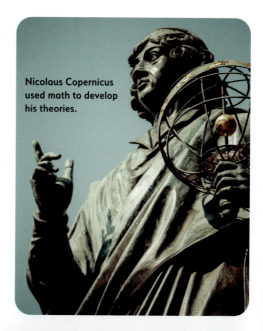

Nicolaus Copernicus used math to develop his theories.

Longer Days

Although each rotation of Earth lasts 24 hours, the amount of daylight on a given day changes. This is due to Earth's axis being angled at 23.5° to point the planet toward or away from the sun at different times of the year. Near the planet's poles, some places experience no daylight or no darkness within a day during particular times of the year.

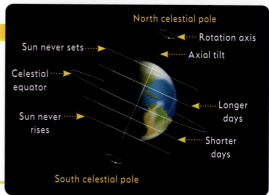

20

A long-exposure photograph shows the path of stars in the night sky as seen from Bishop, California.

EARTH'S ATMOSPHERE

Earth's atmosphere is a mixture of gases, often called air, which is held around Earth by the planet's gravity. Without the atmosphere, there would be no life on Earth. It gives us oxygen and water. The atmosphere acts like a blanket, trapping just enough heat from the sun to keep us warm.

The atmosphere contains around 78 percent nitrogen, 21 percent oxygen, and small amounts of argon, carbon dioxide, and other gases. Moving up through the atmosphere, the air becomes thinner. Scientists divide the atmosphere into layers, depending on their temperature. Although the air generally gets colder farther from Earth, both the thermosphere and stratosphere layers are warmed by energy they absorb from the sun.

LAYERS OF THE ATMOSPHERE

Exosphere

6,200 miles (10,000 km)

Many satellites orbit here.

Thermosphere

430 miles (690 km)

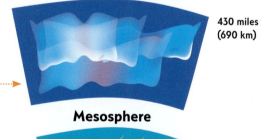

Energy-carrying particles from the sun interact with Earth's magnetic field, creating glowing lights around the poles called auroras.

Mesosphere

53 miles (85 km)

Meteoroids are small rocky or metal bodies that enter Earth's atmosphere, burn up, and create what are known as shooting stars.

Stratosphere

32 miles (50 km)

Weather balloons float in this layer to measure conditions in the atmosphere.

Troposphere

6 miles (10 km)

Airplanes fly among the clouds in the lowest layer.

When the sun heats lakes and oceans, some water evaporates. It turns into a gas called water vapor, which rises in the warm air. As the air rises, it cools. Cold air cannot hold as much evaporated water as warm air, so some of it condenses back into water droplets, which we see as clouds. When the water droplets get too heavy to float, they fall back to Earth as precipitation in the form of rain or snow. This process is called the water cycle.

THE WATER CYCLE

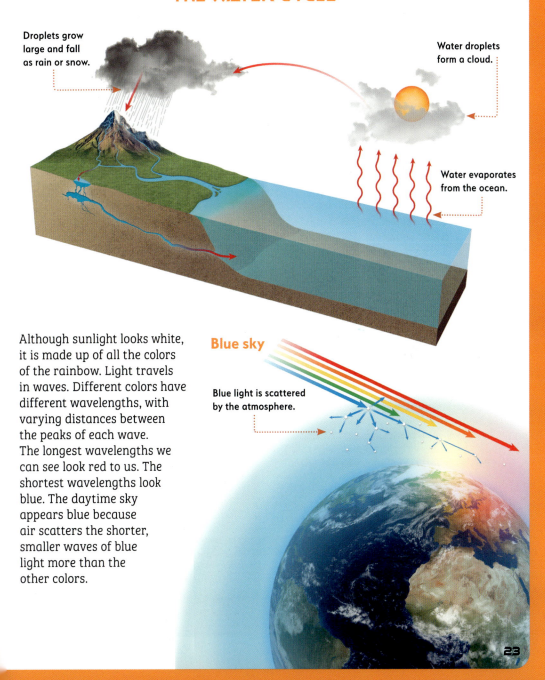

Droplets grow large and fall as rain or snow.

Water droplets form a cloud.

Water evaporates from the ocean.

Blue sky

Blue light is scattered by the atmosphere.

Although sunlight looks white, it is made up of all the colors of the rainbow. Light travels in waves. Different colors have different wavelengths, with varying distances between the peaks of each wave. The longest wavelengths we can see look red to us. The shortest wavelengths look blue. The daytime sky appears blue because air scatters the shorter, smaller waves of blue light more than the other colors.

WATER ON EARTH

Earth's atmosphere, with its unique mixture of gases, makes life on our planet possible. Oxygen is particularly important. It is a vital part of the air we breathe. Oxygen in the ozone shields us from the sun's deadly radiation and excessive heat. When oxygen is combined with carbon in the form of carbon dioxide, it captures and holds just enough of the sun's warmth to make our planet livable. Oxygen also combines with hydrogen to provide Earth's most precious resource—water.

Unlike the other planets in our solar system, Earth has an abundance of liquid water on its surface. Other planets may have ice or water vapor on their surface, or liquid water beneath icy crusts. But almost three-quarters of Earth's surface is covered by water. More than 96 percent of this water is found in the oceans and is too salty to drink. Much of Earth's fresh water is trapped in the planet's ice caps and glaciers. However, there is still enough of it in our lakes, rivers, swamps, and aquifers to sustain billions of humans. It also gives life to Earth's other animals and plants.

All living things depend on the fresh water that falls from the sky as rain or snow. Some of that precipitation is collected in rivers, lakes, and ponds. But most falls on the ground and seeps into the earth where it collects in underground aquifers. Since most of these are found within a half mile (0.8 km) of the surface, humans can access this water by digging wells. There is far more water stored underground than is visible on the surface in lakes and rivers. In fact, freshwater rivers and lakes are primarily fed and refilled by groundwater, not directly by rain or snowfall.

Water World

Earth's total water supply: 326 million trillion gallons (1,234 million trillion L)

Water vapor in the atmosphere: 3,100 cubic miles (12,900 cubic km)

Portion of Earth's surface covered by water: 71 percent

Portion of Earth's water that is salty: 96.5 percent

Portion of fresh water in ice caps and glaciers: 68 percent

Portion of fresh water in the ground: 30 percent

Portion of Earth's total water in rivers: 1/10,000th of 1 percent

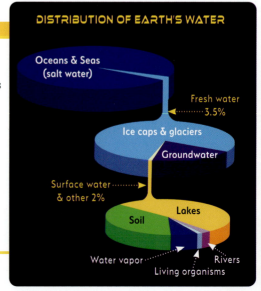

Lake Michigan has a surface area of more than 22,000 square miles (58,000 sq km). It is part of the Great Lakes—the largest freshwater lake system in the world by area, and the second-largest by volume.

LIFE ON EARTH

Very few known planets have the protective atmosphere that has made life on Earth possible. It shields us from radiation, traps warmth, makes the air breathable, and supplies abundant stores of liquid water—all essential for life. Earth supports more than 400,000 plant species, more than 8 billion humans, and about 20 quintillion other animals.

Earth was not always such a hospitable place for life. Early in its history, there was no oxygen. Comets and meteorites that crashed into Earth may have carried amino acids, often called the building blocks of life, to the planet. This may have given rise to microbes that were the only things that could live in such an oxygen-deprived environment. The microbes bound sediment together, creating layered, reef-like structures. Within these organic structures, cyanobacteria developed and began using water and sunlight to create oxygen.

As Earth's oxygen levels increased dramatically, more complex cells emerged and began clustering together to form the planet's first animals. Sponges were among the first creatures to appear, beginning about 800 million years ago. They probably survived by living near the cyanobacteria that produced the oxygen they needed. Soon, frond-shaped sea creatures and wormlike animals began to develop.

Over time, the climate warmed. Oxygen levels began to rise in the ocean as bacteria numbers increased. The warmer temperatures made sea levels rise, and ocean water began moving onto land, creating shallow-water marine habitats that led to an explosion of life. The conditions were perfect for our planet to become a rarity in the galaxy—a home to trillions upon trillions of living things.

The Goldilocks Zone

Out of the thousands of planets we have been able to study with telescopes, Earth remains the only one known to support life. Thanks to its atmosphere's unique combination of gases, we have warmth, air, and liquid water. Part of the reason for this success is that Earth is situated in the Goldilocks zone relative to the sun. We are near enough to keep us warm and covered with lots of liquid water, but far enough away to not be burned up or have all our water evaporate.

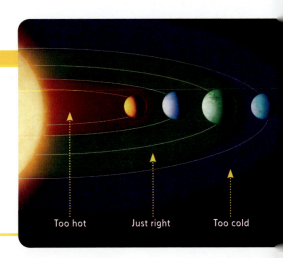

Early life began with simple microbes that were able to survive with little oxygen. Today, these microorganisms are abundant in aquatic environments.

MOON BASICS

Earth has one moon. It is the fifth largest moon in the solar system after ones belonging to Jupiter and Saturn. The moon has orbited our planet for around 4.51 billion years, beginning about 30 million years after Earth formed. The moon follows an elliptical orbit so its distance from Earth ranges between 221,500 miles (356,400 km) and 252,700 miles (406,700 km).

Astronomers believe the moon formed after a Mars-sized planet crashed into the young Earth, sending material shooting into Earth's orbit. This material pulled together to form the moon. The moon has a partly melted core of iron, a mantle of hot rock, and a crust of cool rock. It has almost no atmosphere.

As the moon orbits Earth, it also rotates on an axis. Since the moon takes the same time—27.3 days—to rotate on its axis as it does to travel around Earth, the same side, known as the near side, is always facing Earth. A day on the moon lasts 29.5 Earth days. If an astronaut were standing on the moon, it would take that long for them to see the sun appear to move across the sky and back to its original position.

Because Earth has a significantly tilted axis, its northern and southern hemispheres point toward or away from the sun at certain times of the year, creating seasons. The moon's axis is nearly straight, however, so there are no varying seasons. This also means that some parts of the moon near its poles are in perpetual darkness.

27.3 days to rotate on its axis.

27.3 days to complete one orbit around Earth.

Because the moon's rotation takes the same amount of time as its orbit around Earth, the same side of the moon always faces us.

The Moon

Type: Moon
Size: 2,160 miles (3,476 km) across
Mass: The same as 0.012 Earths
Year: 365.25 Earth days
Day: 29.5 Earth days
Surface temperature: -458 to 260°F (-272 to 127°C)
Average distance from Earth: 238,856 miles (384,402 km)

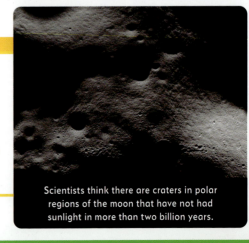

Scientists think there are craters in polar regions of the moon that have not had sunlight in more than two billion years.

The surface of the moon is marked with more than 9,000 craters formed from space objects crashing into it. The bright impact crater to the left of the middle of the moon's near side is called Copernicus.

PHASES OF THE MOON

The moon is the second brightest object in our sky after the sun. This is because it is relatively close and its surface reflects the sun's light. The sun lights up the side of the moon that faces it. Yet, as the moon orbits Earth and Earth orbits the sun, we see different amounts of the moon's bright side. These changes are known as the moon's phases.

When the moon is between the sun and Earth, the sun's light shines on its far side, which we cannot see. From Earth, the moon appears invisible or as a very thin crescent. This is called a new moon. When the moon is on the opposite side of Earth from the sun, sunlight covers the near side. We can see it all from Earth. This is called a full moon. The rest of the time, we see parts of the moon's sunlit face. The cycle repeats every 29.5 days as the moon travels around Earth.

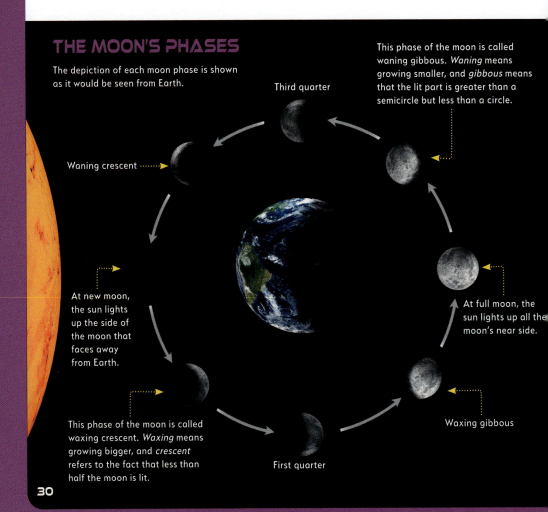

THE MOON'S PHASES

The depiction of each moon phase is shown as it would be seen from Earth.

Third quarter

This phase of the moon is called waning gibbous. *Waning* means growing smaller, and *gibbous* means that the lit part is greater than a semicircle but less than a circle.

Waning crescent

At new moon, the sun lights up the side of the moon that faces away from Earth.

At full moon, the sun lights up all the moon's near side.

Waxing gibbous

This phase of the moon is called waxing crescent. *Waxing* means growing bigger, and *crescent* refers to the fact that less than half the moon is lit.

First quarter

30

A lunar eclipse is when the moon is in Earth's shadow. This happens when the sun, Earth, and moon are in a straight line, with the moon on the opposite side of Earth from the sun. The moon does not go completely dark even during a total eclipse, as it receives some sunlight that has been refracted, or bent, by Earth's atmosphere. A total lunar eclipse happens about twice every three years.

Total lunar eclipse

The moon's face appears reddish during a lunar eclipse. This is because after the sun's light has been bent and scattered, only the wavelengths that we see as red remain.

In a solar eclipse, the moon blocks the face of the sun. This happens when the sun, moon, and Earth are exactly lined up. Total solar eclipses last for a few minutes and can be seen from somewhere on Earth around once every 18 months. Looking directly at the sun can cause blindness, so a solar eclipse should never be watched directly or through a camera.

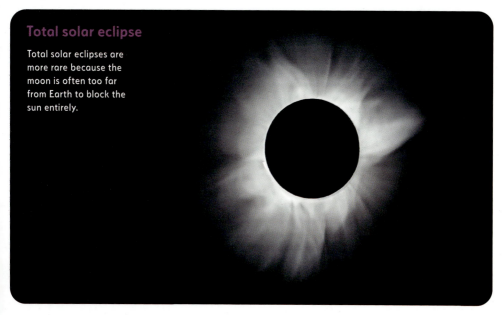

Total solar eclipse

Total solar eclipses are more rare because the moon is often too far from Earth to block the sun entirely.

THE LUNAR SURFACE

Gazing at the full moon, we see gray areas within the shining orb. Astronomers once believed the dark areas were water-filled seas surrounded by lighter-colored plains. Only after Italian astronomer Galileo Galilei studied the moon through one of the first telescopes did we learn that the darker areas were volcanic craters and the lighter spots were rugged and mountainous.

How did this strange lunar landscape form? After an object the size of Mars collided with Earth about 4.5 billion years ago, the impact sheared off part of Earth's mantle and crust. Some of this superheated debris clumped together and formed the moon. At this time, the moon was just a massive ocean of magma surrounding a solid core. As the magma cooled, it sank below the surface. The moon ultimately became structured in a way similar to Earth—a molten iron core, a mantle of partially melted rock, and a rocky crust of solid rock.

About half a billion years after the moon's fiery birth, its cooling surface was bombarded by thousands of meteors and other space objects. The tall edges of the impact craters and basins formed the moon's mountainous, brighter areas we see from Earth. The craters can be as many as 8 miles (13 km) below the moon's average surface height, while the peaks can rise as much as 3 miles (4.8 km) above the average.

Some meteor strikes punctured the moon's crust, releasing magma, which flowed upward to flood the impact craters and create flat plains of basalt. A plain on the moon is called a mare, Latin for sea. These lunar landforms are the dark gray areas we see that were once believed to contain water. Meteors continue to strike the moon and reshape its surface today, though with far less frequency than in the past.

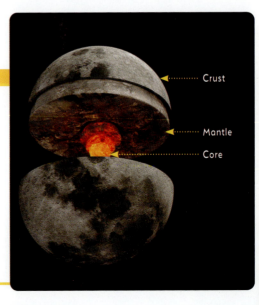

Surface Details

Average depth of the moon's crust: 42 miles (68 km)

Average depth of the moon's mantle: 825 miles (1,330 km)

Number of craters wider than 0.6 miles (1 km) on the moon's near side: 300,000

Largest crater on the moon: The South Pole-Aitken Basin; 1,390 miles (2,240 km) in diameter and 8.1 miles (13 km) deep

Largest mare or plain: Mare Imbrium; 700 miles (1,100 km) in diameter

Average depth of a mare: About 1.8 miles (3 km)

When scientists first identified the markings on the moon's surface, they thought they came from either meteor impacts, volcanic eruptions, or glacial movement. Today, scientists know that all lunar craters were created by impacts from space objects.

THE MOON'S ATMOSPHERE

When we observe the moon's scarred surface with thousands of craters, basins, volcanic plains, and mountainous highlands, it is easy to wonder why Earth has not been similarly marked by meteors. The answer lies in the moon's atmosphere—or lack of one.

It was once thought that the moon had no atmosphere at all. There is no air, no breezes, and no weather on the moon. The surface appears still and unchanging. But scientists have discovered that the moon does, indeed, have a very thin layer of gases that make up an exosphere. The gases in it are so spread out that their molecules almost never collide with one another. While Earth's atmosphere has about 100 quintillion molecules per cubic centimeter (0.06 cubic in.), the moon's has only 100 molecules in the same volume of space. This makes the moon's atmosphere 10 trillion times thinner than Earth's.

How does this affect the moon's surface? The moon's exosphere is far too thin to protect it from incoming meteors. On Earth, the atmosphere can deflect or burn up meteors before they reach the surface, but the moon's atmosphere offers no defense. Since there is so little atmosphere on the moon, resulting in a lack of wind, water, and weather, there is also no erosion. Once a mark is made on the moon's soil, it will remain as it is until disturbed again by another outside object. On Earth, erosion of land and tectonic plate activity have erased many of Earth's impact craters from the past. But we can see evidence of nearly every strike on the moon's surface, even those made by objects as small as a human blood cell!

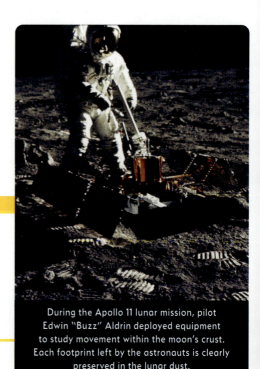

During the Apollo 11 lunar mission, pilot Edwin "Buzz" Aldrin deployed equipment to study movement within the moon's crust. Each footprint left by the astronauts is clearly preserved in the lunar dust.

Mystery Gases

The moon's exosphere has oxygen, carbon dioxide, and helium. However, the origin of those gases is mysterious. They may have been released from the moon's interior during moonquakes, volcanic eruptions, or rock decay. They may also have been brought by meteors. Scientists think sunlight and meteor strikes can release gases buried in the moon's soil.

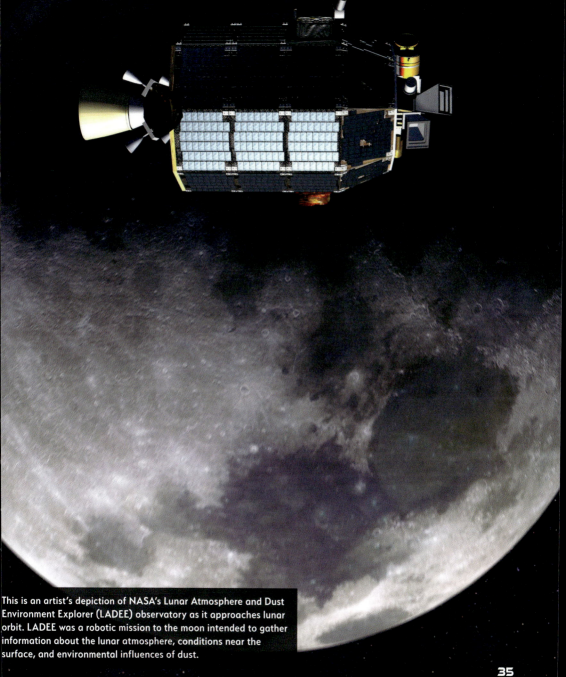

This is an artist's depiction of NASA's Lunar Atmosphere and Dust Environment Explorer (LADEE) observatory as it approaches lunar orbit. LADEE was a robotic mission to the moon intended to gather information about the lunar atmosphere, conditions near the surface, and environmental influences of dust.

THE MOON AND EARTH'S TIDES

When you spend a day at the beach, you may notice the water moving farther inland or retreating back toward the sea. The size of the exposed part of the beach changes over the course of several hours. On different days, the water level changes at different times and to varying extents. When the water has fully retreated, it is known as low tide. When it has come as far onto land as it can, it is high tide.

What causes this alternation between low and high tides? The answer is not in the waves but in the sky. The moon is much smaller than Earth, with a mass equal to only 1 percent of our planet's. Yet the moon is still close enough and massive enough to exert a strong gravitational force upon Earth. Its pull is so strong, in fact, that it actually stretches Earth slightly, making it squish at the poles and bulge at the equator.

High tide

Solar Tides

The sun also plays a role in tides. Twice a month, the sun, moon, and Earth line up, creating a large gravitational pull that causes unusually high tides, known as spring tides. A week after each spring tide, the moon and sun are at right angles to each other, causing their gravitational pulls to work against each other. The low gravitational pull at this time creates neap tides—very moderate tides with less difference between the highest and lowest water levels.

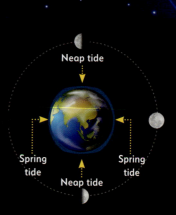

The tidal bulge created by the moon changes as the moon orbits Earth. When the moon's tidal bulge aligns with the sun's, the extreme tides known as spring tides occur.

36

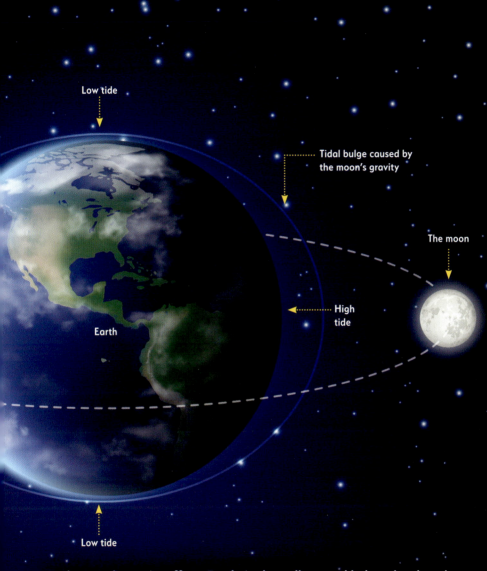

As the moon's gravity affects Earth, it also pulls on and bulges the planet's ocean water. The seas on the sides of the planet that are closest to and farthest from the moon at any particular time are pushed outward, causing high tide. Meanwhile, the seas that are on the two sides of Earth that are neither closest to nor farthest from the moon at the time contract, or are squeezed inward. This is low tide. Most coasts have two low and two high tides per day. Each high and low tide is separated by about 12 hours.

LANDING ON THE MOON

For hundreds of thousands of years, humans have looked up at the moon and wondered what it would be like to walk on and explore its surface. For most of that time, the idea was merely a dream. With the invention of the modern rocket in 1926, it suddenly seemed possible that humans would someday travel to the moon.

Forty-three years later, after decades of research, experimentation, failed launches, and test space flights, this dream became a reality. On July 20, 1969, the Apollo 11 mission landed U.S. astronauts Neil Armstrong and Edwin "Buzz" Aldrin on the moon, while Michael Collins waited aboard their command and service module orbiting the moon. Armstrong and Aldrin were the first and second humans to set foot on the moon.

The mission began on July 16, when the spacecraft, carrying the three astronauts, was blasted into Earth's orbit by a Saturn V rocket. On July 20, Armstrong and Aldrin undocked the lunar module from the command and service module and flew down to the lunar surface. They spent 21 hours and 36 minutes on the moon, taking photographs, doing experiments, and collecting rock samples.

For the first time in human history, people had left their home planet, traveled beyond Earth's atmosphere into outer space, and walked upon another space body. After the first moon landing, there were several other Apollo missions and moon landings. This launched humankind into a new era of space exploration.

Moon Mission Numbers

Manned moon landings: 6
Astronauts traveled to the moon: 24
Astronauts walked on the moon: 12
Astronauts traveled to the moon twice: 3
Total time humans spent on the lunar surface: 80 hours and 28 minutes

During the first moonwalk, the astronauts and equipment were being closely monitored by NASA workers at the Mission Control Center.

Astronaut Buzz Aldrin takes his first step onto the surface of the moon.

WALKING ON THE MOON

What was it like to walk on the moon? Buzz Aldrin described what he saw all around him as "magnificent desolation." The mare in which they landed was almost completely flat, with nothing between the astronauts and the horizon. The moon was awe-inspiring in its stark beauty but also eerie in its gray stillness and silence.

The gray soil and the dark shadows cast by the crater walls of the moon's highlands make it look frigid. But on the bright side of the moon where Aldrin and other Apollo astronauts landed, it was very hot—about 200°F (93°C). And though the gray surface looks soft and powdery, it is actually composed of dust, sharp rock fragments, and shards of volcanic glass. It could wear away and rip the spacesuits that protected the astronauts from the extreme conditions and supplied them with oxygen.

The moon's gravity is about one-sixth that of Earth's, which means that on the moon things weigh less. The Apollo astronauts were not weightless on the moon, but their bodies were far lighter than on Earth because there was less pull from gravity.

The astronauts found that hopping was an easier way to move around on the moon than walking.

Because the moon's surface is made of rocky and glassy debris, it is very reflective. It is extremely bright when the sun shines on it. This reflected light obscures the stars above the moon, so the sky looks completely black. The astronauts could, however, see Earth directly above their heads. For the first time in human history, individuals were looking up to gaze at Earth, while people back on Earth were simultaneously gazing up at the moon.

Astronaut Alan B. Shepard standing with an American flag on the lunar surface in 1971

Flapless Flags

Because there is almost no atmosphere on the moon, the U.S. flags planted by Apollo astronauts did not flap or billow. They had to be attached to a horizontal tube along the top to make them fully visible. More than 50 years later, most of the flags continue to stand. Their nylon fabric has probably been bleached white by the sunlight and radiation that the moon's thin atmosphere is unable to block.

In 1972, Apollo 16 commander John W. Young collected rock samples at the North Ray Crater geological site. The Lunar Roving Vehicle behind Young traveled a total of 16.6 miles (26.7 km) in 3 hours and 26 minutes of driving during the mission.

SIDE BY SIDE

The fact that there is life on Earth is extraordinary. The planet wraps us within a thick atmosphere that protects against extreme cold and heat. It blocks out harmful energy. Our planet contains an abundance of water within its massive stores of oceans, lakes, rivers, and underground aquifers thanks to these gases. Without this water, life of any kind would be impossible. The minerals and gases locked within Earth's soil, sand, rocks, and mountains provide the elements needed for life to grow, develop, and reproduce.

When we look up at the night sky from Earth and gaze at the large white object glowing above us, we have a constant companion in the moon. Even on those nights when we were not able to see it, it has been there, always orbiting around us. We feel its presence in the rising and falling tides, even when its light is darkened. Every day and night for the last 4.5 billion years, the moon has circled Earth.

When humans first set down on the lunar surface, Earth and the moon became even closer. They were now linked by life—human beings had traveled on both spheres, gazing at the other with feet on planetary and lunar soils. Earth and the moon will continue their journey through space, side by side, for billions of years. And humans will continue to stand in awe of Earth's beauty and bounty, as we bask in the moon's watchful glow.

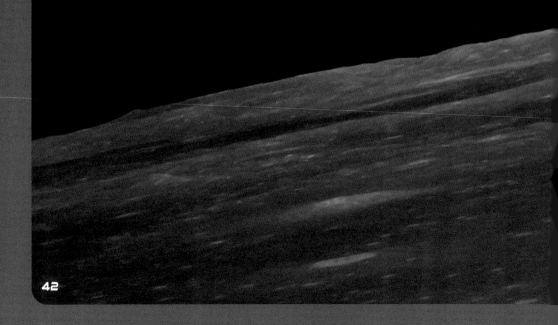

This view from the Apollo 11 spacecraft shows Earth rising above the moon's horizon.

REVIEW AND REFLECT

Now that you've read about Earth and the moon, let's review what you've learned. Use the following questions to reflect on your newfound knowledge and integrate it with what you already knew.

Check for Understanding

1. Describe Earth's axis. In what way is the axis related to Earth's rotation? *(See p. 6)*

2. When did Earth form? How much later did Earth's moon form? *(See p. 8)*

3. Name and describe each of Earth's four layers. *(See p. 10)*

4. Describe two things that can happen when tectonic plates meet and make contact with one another. *(See p. 12)*

5. What was Pangea and what happened to it? *(See p. 14)*

6. How does Earth's magnetic field protect the planet? *(See p. 16)*

7. During the summer solstice, what is happening with Earth's axis? What is happening on Earth? What about during the spring and fall equinoxes? *(See pp. 18–19)*

8. Why is one day on Earth 24 hours? *(See pp. 20–21)*

9. Name the four layers of Earth's atmosphere and give an example of something that happens in each. *(See pp. 22–23)*

10. What is oxygen and why is it important? *(See pp. 24–25)*

11. How has Earth changed over time? *(See p. 26)*

12. Why is a day on the moon longer than a day on Earth? *(See pp. 28–29)*

13. What are the moon's phases? Why do they happen? *(See pp. 30–31)*

14. Describe two events that made the moon's surface the way it is. *(See pp. 32–33)*

15. What causes high and low tides? *(See pp. 36–37)*

Making Connections

1. How does Earth's axis affect the number of daylight hours people experience? How does it affect temperature?

2. How do astronomers think Earth's moon formed? How did it change over time?

3. List at least three characteristics of Earth that make life possible on the planet.

4. In what ways are Earth's atmosphere and the moon's exosphere different?

5. Describe the surface of the moon. How is it different from Earth's surface?

In Your Own Words

1. Why do you think humans wanted to travel to the moon? Would you want to go to the moon? Why or why not?

2. Scientists think that someday tectonic plates may come together again. How do you think that would change life on Earth?

3. What can people learn from studying the moon? Why is this work important or valuable?

4. Some people want to start colonies on the moon. Imagine what that might be like. How would living on the moon be different from living on Earth?

5. If you were to assign human traits to both Earth and the moon, which traits would you choose? Why?

GLOSSARY

astronomer a scientist who studies the planets, stars, and other objects in space

atmosphere the gases surrounding a planet or moon, held by its gravity

atom the smallest unit of matter; an atom has a nucleus with protons and neutrons, usually surrounded by one or more electrons

axis an imaginary line through a planet or moon, around which the object rotates

core the inner region of a planet or moon

crust the outer layer of a planet or moon

eclipse when a body, such as a star, planet, or moon, is obscured by passing into the shadow of another body or by having another body pass between it and the viewer

galaxy millions or billions of stars, as well as gas and dust, that are held together by gravity

gas a substance that is not solid, liquid, or plasma; gas will expand to fill any container

gravity the force that pulls all objects and particles toward one another

helium the second most common and second lightest element in the universe

hemisphere half of a sphere, such as that of a planet or moon

hydrogen the most common and lightest element in the universe

impact crater a bowl-shaped dip caused by a collision with an asteroid or other body

magnetism a force caused by the movement of an electric charge, resulting in pulling and pushing forces between objects

mantle the layer inside a planet or moon that lies between the core and the crust

mass a measure of the amount of matter in an object

matter a physical substance, in the form of a solid, liquid, gas, or plasm

microbes single-celled organisms

molecule a group of atoms that are bonded together

moon a round object that orbits a planet

orbit the curved path of an object around a star, planet, or moon

oxygen the third most common element in the universe

particle a tiny portion of matter

robotic relating to a machine programmed to carry out some of its activities independently

solar system the sun along with all the planets and other objects in orbit around it

READ MORE

Hulick, Kathryn. *The Night Sky (Field Guides for Kids).* Minneapolis: ABDO Reference, 2022.

Light, Charlie. *Observing Earth: Investigating Earth's Atmosphere (Liftoff! Space Exploration).* New York: Gareth Stevens Publishing, 2021.

Miller, Ron. *Natural Satellites: The Book of Moons.* Minneapolis: Twenty-First Century Books, 2021.

Wiseman, Blaine. *Earth and the Moon (Space Systems: Stars and the Solar System).* New York: Lightbox/Smartbook Media, 2021.

LEARN MORE ONLINE

1. Go to **www.factsurfer.com** or scan the QR code below.
2. Enter **"Earth and Moon"** into the search box.
3. Click on the cover of this book to see a list of websites.

47

INDEX

Aldrin, Edwin "Buzz" 34, 38–40
Apollo missions 34, 38, 40–41, 43
Armstrong, Neil 38
astronauts 28, 34, 38, 40
atmosphere 9, 16–17, 22–24, 26, 28, 31, 34–35, 38, 40, 42
aurora 17
axis 6, 16, 18, 20, 28
Collins, Michael 38
comets 26
Copernicus, Nicolaus 20, 29
core 6, 8, 10, 16, 28, 32
craters 28–29, 32–34, 40
crust 6, 8, 10–13, 28, 32, 34
eclipses 31
Galilei, Galileo 32
Goldilocks Zone 26
gravity 8, 22, 40
Jupiter 28
life 4, 6, 8, 16, 22, 24, 26, 42
light 4, 8, 17, 23, 30–31, 40, 42
Lunar Atmosphere and Dust Environment Explorer 35
Lunar Reconnaissance Orbiter 7
lunar roving vehicles 41
magnetic field 16–17, 22
mantle 10, 12, 14, 28, 32
Mars 8, 16, 28, 32
moon phases 30
moon, the 4–8, 28–40, 42–43
NASA 35, 38
orbit 4, 6, 8, 18–19, 22, 28, 35, 38
oxygen 16–17, 22, 24, 26–27, 34, 40
Pangea 14–15
satellites 22
Saturn 28, 38–39
seasons 6, 19–20, 28
Shepard, Alan B. 40
solar winds 16–17
spacecraft 7, 38, 43
stars 6, 8, 20, 22, 40
sun, the 17, 19, 20
tectonic plates 6, 12–14, 34
telescopes 26
Theia 8
tides 36–37, 42, 44
water 6, 9, 16, 22–24, 26, 32, 34, 36–37, 42
water cycle 23
Young, John W. 41